the Beach Boys for UKULELE

ISBN 978-1-4234-9643-4

HAL•LEONARD®
CORPORATION

7777 W. BLUEMOUND RD. P.O. BOX 13819 MILWAUKEE, WI 53213

Visit Hal Leonard Online at
www.halleonard.com

Barbara Ann

Words and Music by Fred Fassert

Be True to Your School

Words and Music by Brian Wilson and Mike Love

Chorus

just like you would to your girl ___ or guy. ___ Be true to your school ___ now ___ and let your col - ors fly. ___ Be true to your school. ___

1., 2.

3.
Outro

2. I got a
3. On

So be true to your school.

So be true to your school. ___

California Girls

Words and Music by Brian Wilson and Mike Love

First note

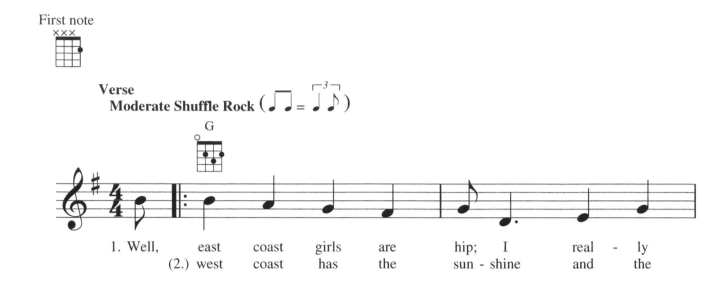

Verse
Moderate Shuffle Rock

1. Well, east coast girls are hip; I real - ly
(2.) west coast has the sun - shine and the

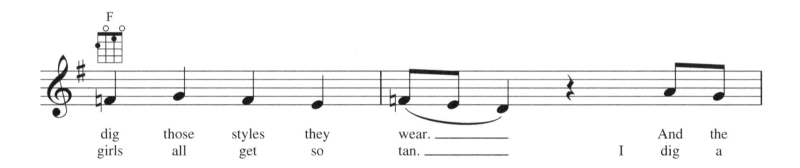

dig those styles they wear. _____ And the
girls all get so tan. _____ I dig a

south - ern girls ___ with ___ the way they talk, ___ they knock me
French bi - ki - ni on Ha - wai - ian is - lands, ___ dolls by a

out when I'm down there. ___ The mid - west farm - er's
palm tree in the sand. ___ I been all a - round this

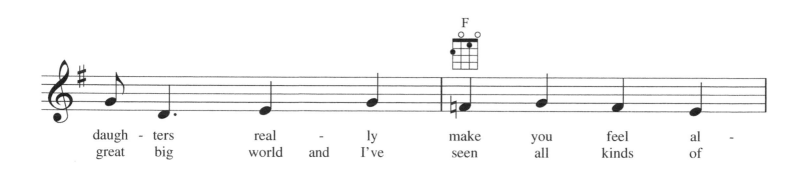

daugh - ters real - ly make you feel al -
great big world and I've seen all kinds of

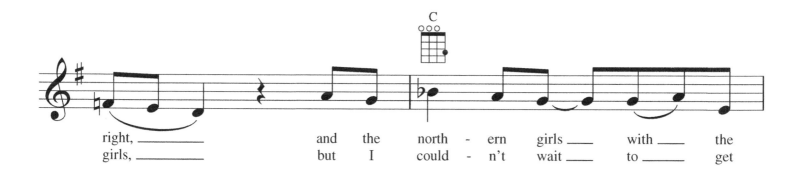

right, _____ and the north - ern girls _____ with _____ the
girls, _____ but I could - n't wait _____ to _____ get

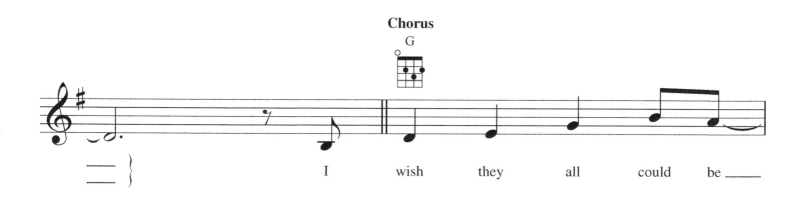

way they kiss, ___ they keep their boy - friends warm at night. ___
back in the states, ___ back to the cut - est girls in the world. ___

Chorus

I wish they all could be _____

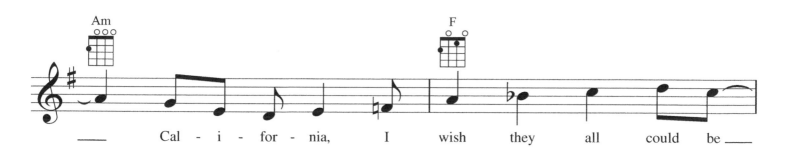

_____ Cal - i - for - nia, I wish they all could be _____

7

Cal - i - for - nia, I wish they all could be ____

1.

____ Cal - i - for - nia girls. _____ 2. The

2.

Interlude

N.C.

girls. _____ *(Instrumental)*

Outro-Chorus

I wish they all could be ____

1.

____ Cal - i - for - nia, wish they all could be ____ Cal - i - for - nia, I

2.

____ Cal - i - for - nia girls. _____

Fun, Fun, Fun

Words and Music by Brian Wilson and Mike Love

Chorus

now. _____
now. _____

And she'll have fun, fun, fun, till her

dad-dy takes the T-Bird a-way. _____

1.

2. Well, the

2.

Verse

3. A-well, you knew all a-long ___ that your

dad was get-tin' wise to you _____ now. _____

And since he took your set of keys, you've been

think-in' that your fun is all through ___ now. _____

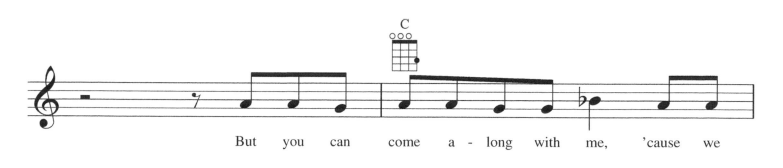

But you can come a - long with me, 'cause we

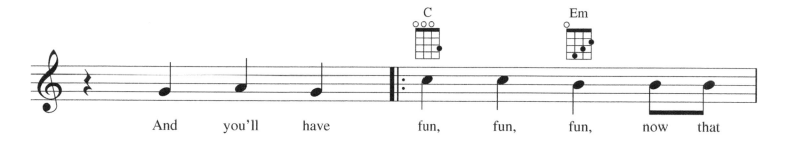

got - ta lot - ta things to do _____ now. _____

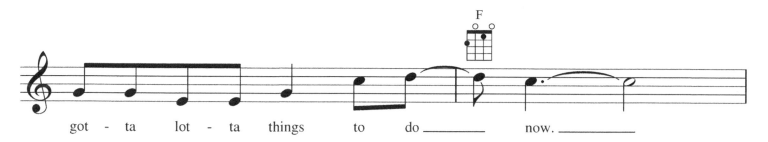

And you'll have fun, fun, fun, now that

dad - dy took the T - Bird a - way. _____

1. And you'll have

2. And you'll have fun, fun, fun, now that

Outro-Chorus

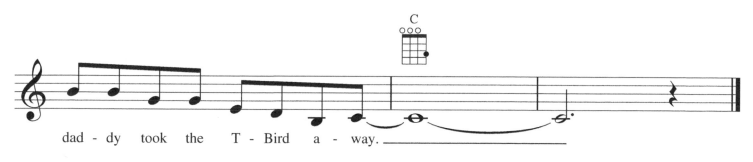

dad - dy took the T - Bird a - way. _____

Dance, Dance, Dance

Words and Music by Brian Wilson, Carl Wilson and Mike Love

First note

Verse
Moderate Rock

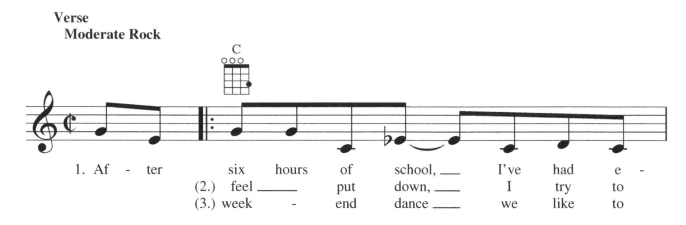

1. Af - ter six hours of school, ___ I've had e -
(2.) feel _____ put down, ___ I try to
(3.) week - end dance ___ we like to

nough for the day. ___ I hit the ra - di - o dial ___ and turn it
shake it off quick. ___ With my chick by my side, ___ the ra - di -
show ___ up last. ___ I play it cool when it's slow ___ and jump

Chorus

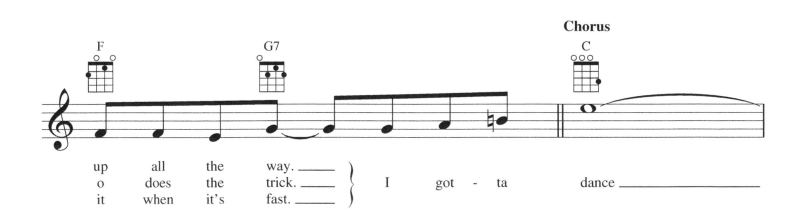

up all the way. ___ ⎫
o does the trick. ___ ⎬ I got - ta dance _____
it when it's fast. ___ ⎭

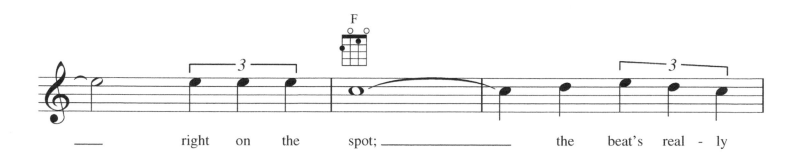

right on the spot; _____ the beat's real - ly

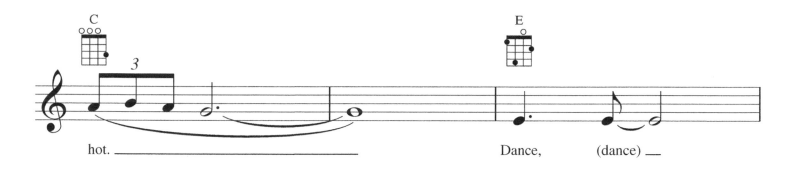

hot. _____ Dance, (dance) _

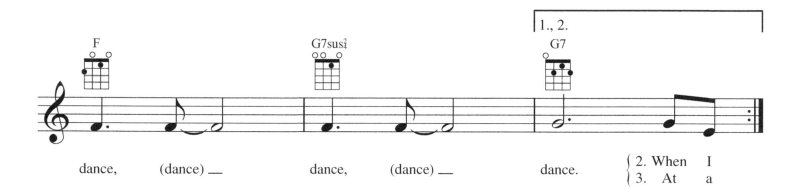

dance, (dance) _ dance, (dance) _ dance.

{ 2. When I
{ 3. At a

Outro-Chorus

3.

dance. Dance, (dance) _ dance, (dance) _

Optional Ending

Repeat and Fade

dance, (dance) _ dance.

Darlin'

Words and Music by Brian Wilson and Mike Love

First note

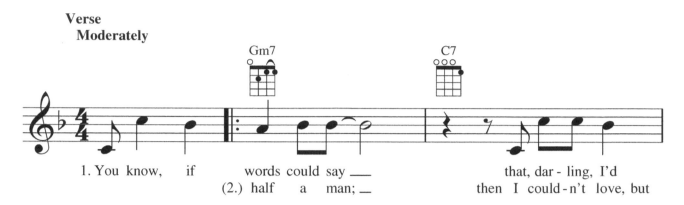

Verse
Moderately

1. You know, if words could say ___ that, dar - ling, I'd
(2.) half a man; ___ then I could-n't love, but

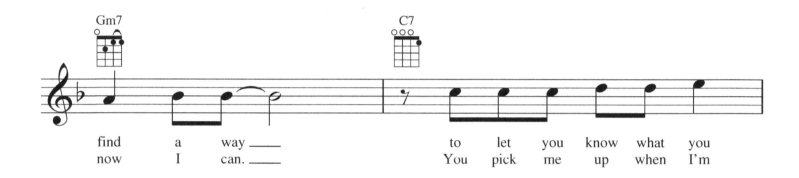

find a way ___ to let you know what you
now I can. ___ You pick me up when I'm

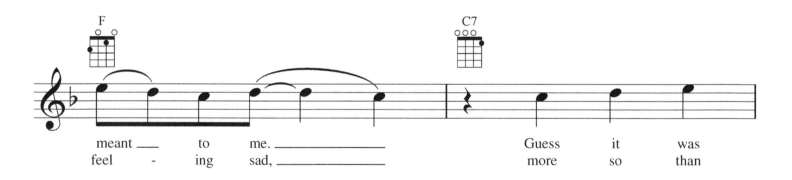

meant ___ to me. ___ Guess it was
feel - ing sad, ___ more so than

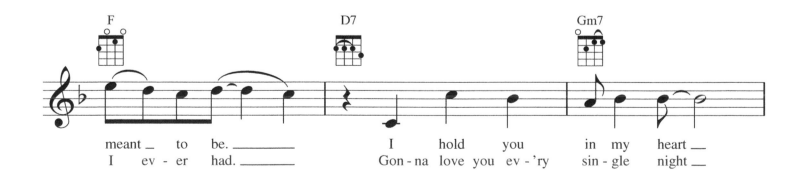

meant _ to be. ___ I hold you in my heart ___
I ev - er had. ___ Gon - na love you ev - 'ry sin - gle night ___

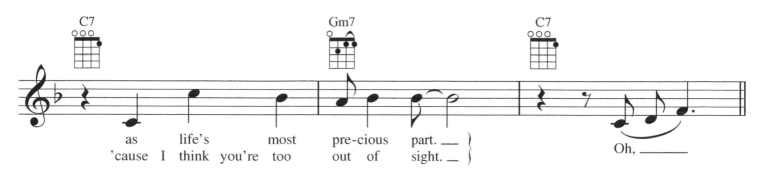

as   life's   most   pre-cious   part. ___
'cause I think you're too   out of   sight. ___

Oh, _____

𝄋 **Chorus**

dar - lin', _____   I   dream a - bout you of - ten,   my ___

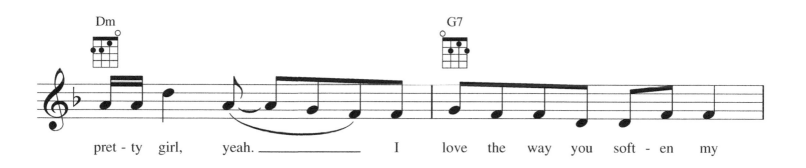

pret - ty girl,   yeah. _____   I   love   the   way   you   soft - en   my

life with your love, __   your   pre-cious love,   uh - huh. _____

Coda ⊕

1.
C7

2.
C7

D.S. al Coda

⊕ **Coda**
F

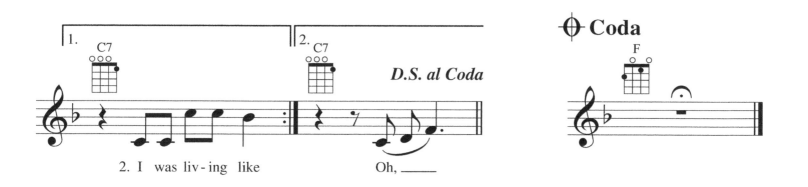

2. I was liv-ing like   Oh, _____

Don't Worry Baby

Words and Music by Brian Wilson and Roger Christian

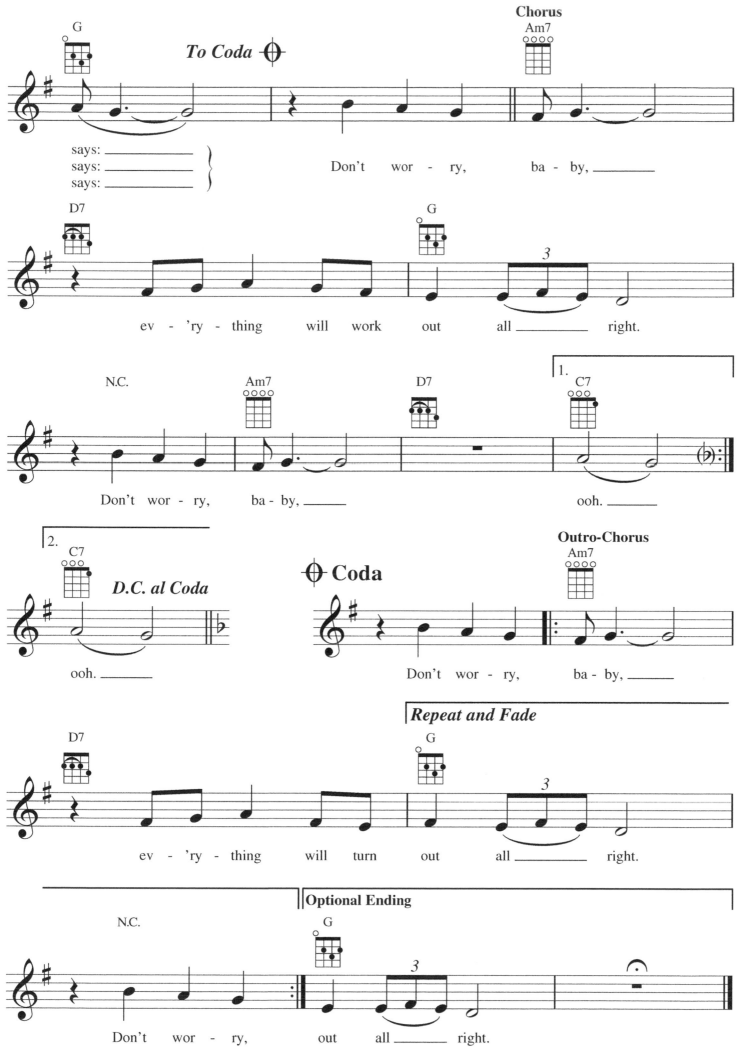

God Only Knows

Words and Music by Brian Wilson and Tony Asher

First note

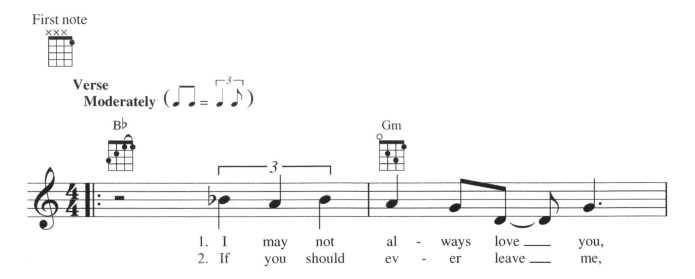

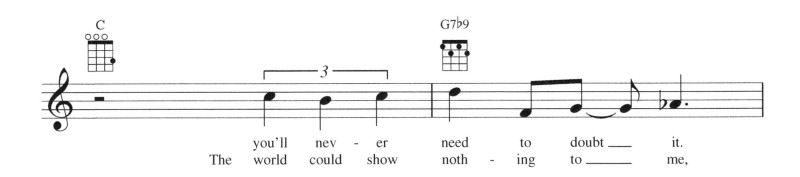

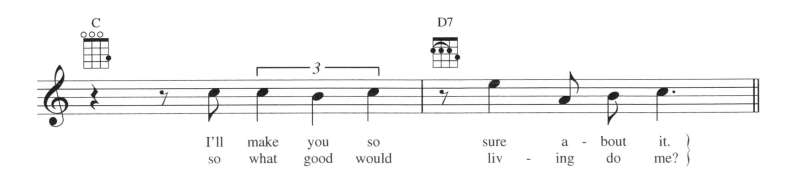

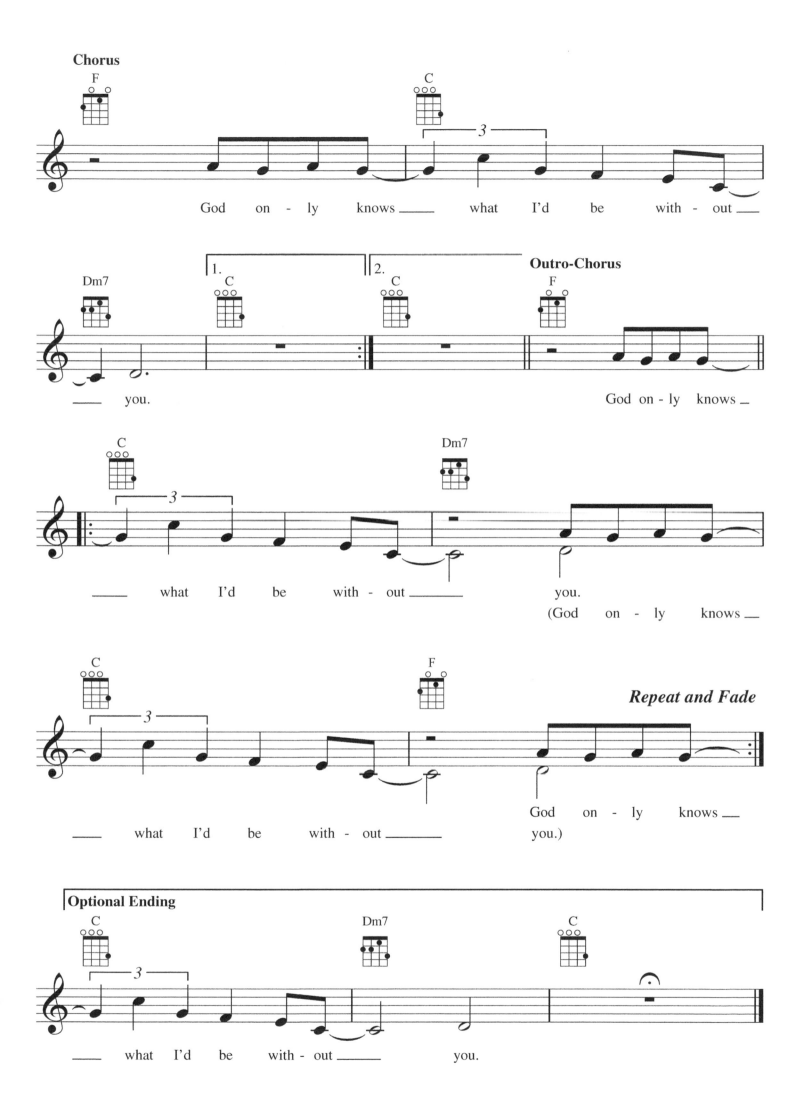

Good Vibrations

Words and Music by Brian Wilson and Mike Love

First note

Verse
Moderately fast

1. I, _____ I love the col - or - ful
2. Close my eyes; she's __ some - how

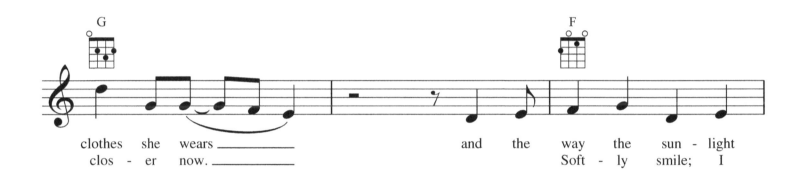

clothes she wears _____ and the way the sun - light
clos - er now. _____ Soft - ly smile; I

plays up - on __ her hair. _____
know she must __ be kind. _____

I _____ hear the sound of a gen - tle word _____
When _____ I look in her eyes, _____

on the wind that lifts her per - fume through the air. _____

she goes with me to a blos - som _____ world. _

Chorus

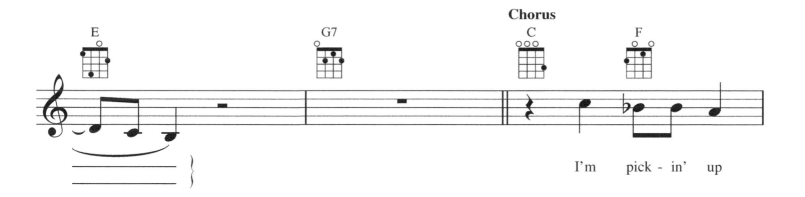

I'm pick - in' up

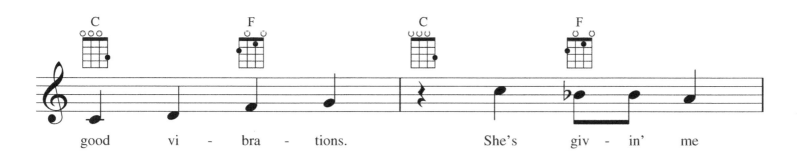

good vi - bra - tions. She's giv - in' me

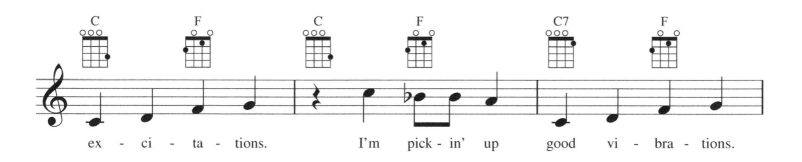

ex - ci - ta - tions. I'm pick - in' up good vi - bra - tions.

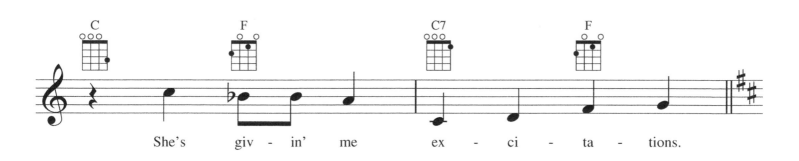

She's giv - in' me ex - ci - ta - tions.

Interlude

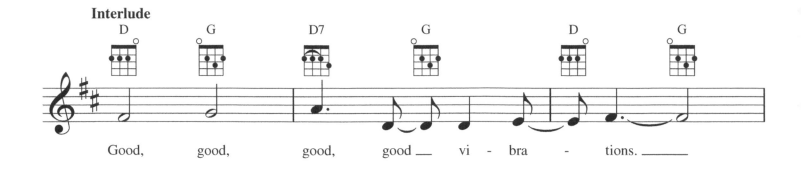

Good, good, good, good _ vi - bra - tions. _____

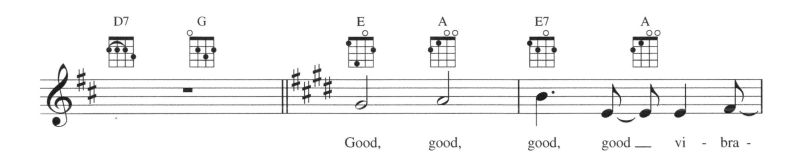

Good, good, good, good _ vi - bra -

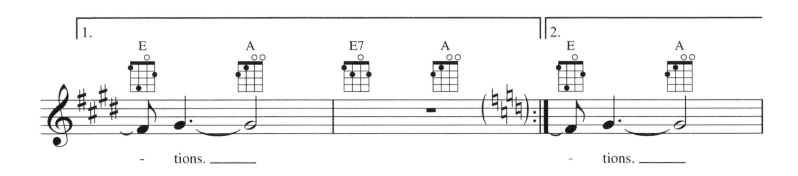

1.   - tions. _____   2.   - tions. _____

Outro-Chorus

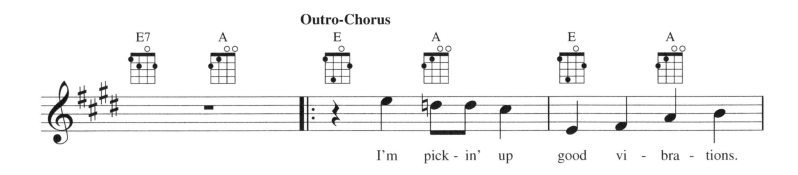

I'm pick - in' up good vi - bra - tions.

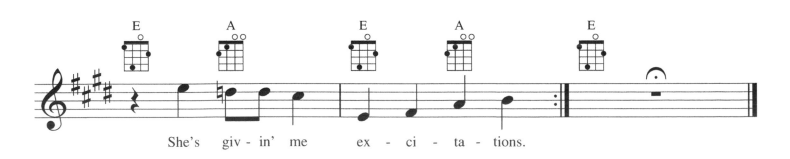

She's giv - in' me ex - ci - ta - tions.

Help Me Rhonda

Words and Music by Brian Wilson and Mike Love

First note

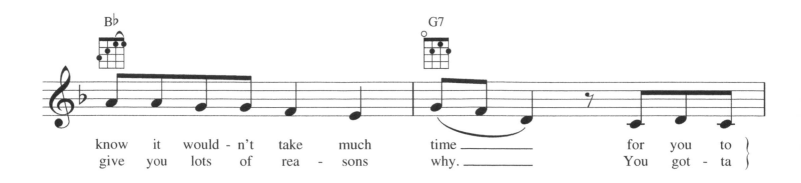

know it would-n't take much time _____ for you to

give you lots of rea - sons why. _____ You got-ta

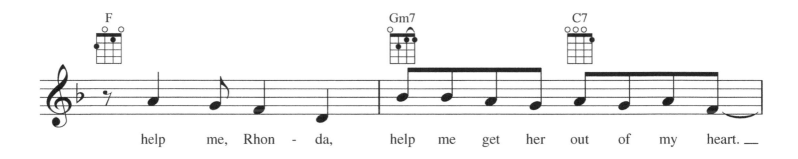

help me, Rhon - da, help me get her out of my heart. _

Chorus

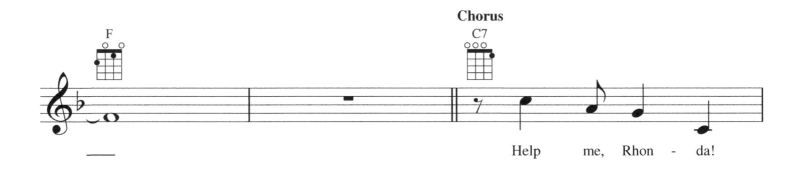

_ Help me, Rhon - da!

Help, help me, Rhon - da! Help me, Rhon - da! Help, help me, Rhon - da!

Help me, Rhon - da! Help, help me, Rhon - da! Help me, Rhon - da!

Help, help me, Rhon - da! Help me, Rhon - da! Help, help me, Rhon - da!

Help me, Rhon - da! Help, help me, Rhon - da! Help me, Rhon - da,

1.

yeah, get her out of my heart. _____ 2. She was

2.

Outro-Chorus

_____ Help me, Rhon - da! Help, help me, Rhon - da!

Optional Ending

Repeat and Fade

Help me, Rhon - da! Help, help me, Rhon - da!

I Get Around

Words and Music by Brian Wilson and Mike Love

My
None of the

bud - dies and me ____ are get - tin' real well - known. ___ Yeah, the
guys ___ go stead - y 'cause it would - n't be right ___ to leave your

bad guys know us and they leave us a - lone. ___ } I get a -
best girl home ___ on a Sat - ur - day night. ___ }

Chorus

round _____ from ___ town to town. _____

____ I'm a real cool head; _____ I'm mak - in' real good bread. __

_____ 2. We ___

In My Room

Words and Music by Brian Wilson and Gary Usher

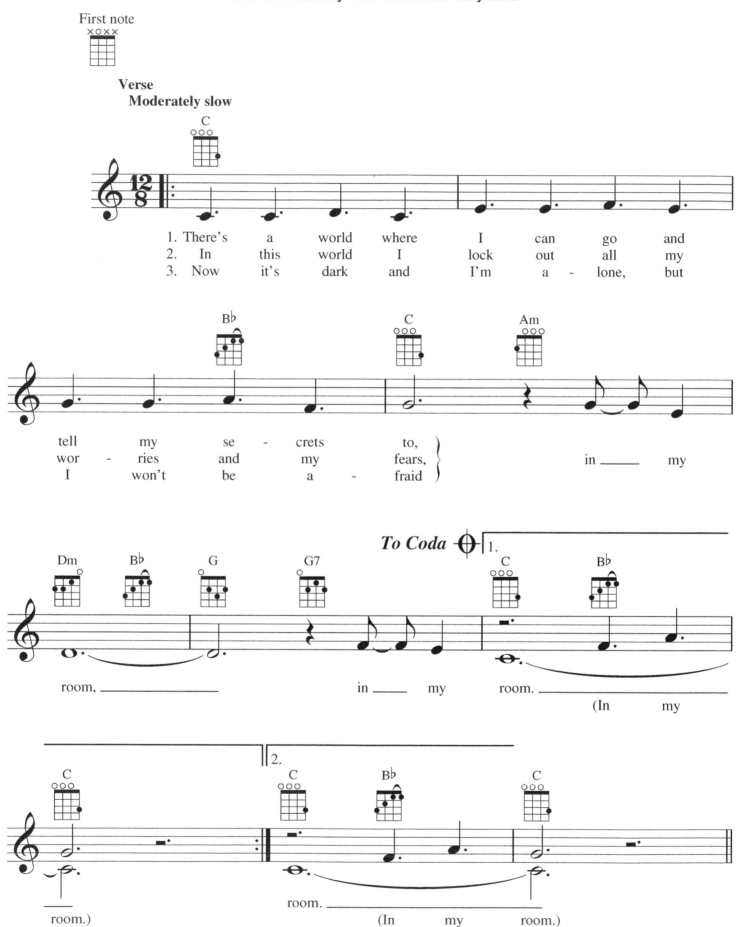

Bridge

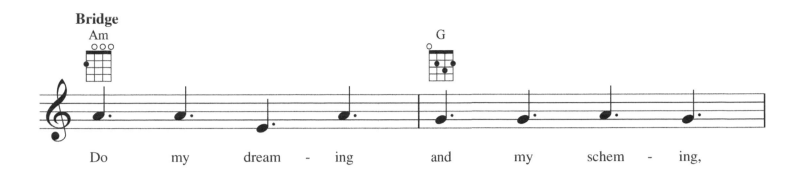

Do my dream - ing and my schem - ing,

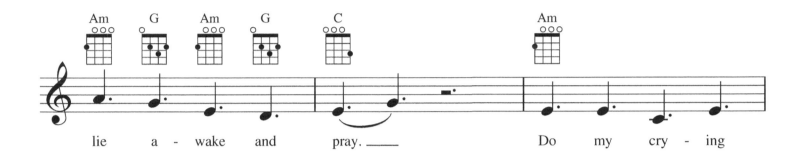

lie a - wake and pray. _____ Do my cry - ing

D.C. al Coda

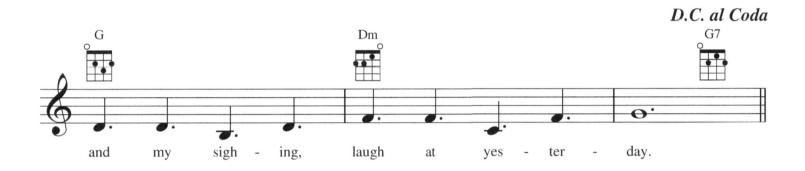

and my sigh - ing, laugh at yes - ter - day.

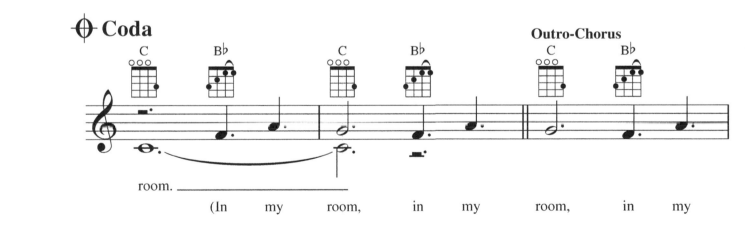

⊕ **Coda**

Outro-Chorus

room. _____ (In my room, in my room, in my

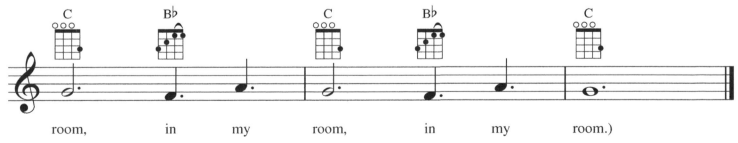

room, in my room, in my room.)

Kokomo
from the Motion Picture COCKTAIL

Words and Music by Mike Love, Terry Melcher, John Phillips and Scott McKenzie

want to go ____ to get a - way from it all. ____
____ a lit - tle bit of grav - i - ty. ____

Verse

Bod - ies in the sand, ____ trop - i - cal drink melt - ing
Af - ter - noon de - light, ____ cock - tails and

in your hand. ____ We'll be fall - ing in love ____ to the rhy - thm of a
moon-lit nights, _ the dream-y look in your eye, ____ give me a trop - i - cal

𝄋 Chorus

steel - drum band ____ down in Ko - ko - mo.⎫ A - ru - ba, Ja - mai - ca, ooh, _
con - tact high ____ way down in Ko - ko - mo.⎭

____ I wan - na take ya to Ber - mu - da, Ba - ha - ma. Come ____

____ on, pret - ty ma - ma. Key Lar - go, Mon - te - go, ba - by, why don't we go down to

Wouldn't It Be Nice

Words and Music by Brian Wilson, Tony Asher and Mike Love

Oh, would-n't it ___ be _____ nice? _____

Chorus
Slower

You know, it seems the more we talk a - bout ___ it,

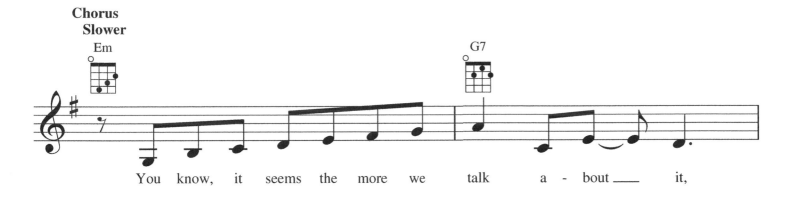

it on - ly makes it worse to live with - out ___

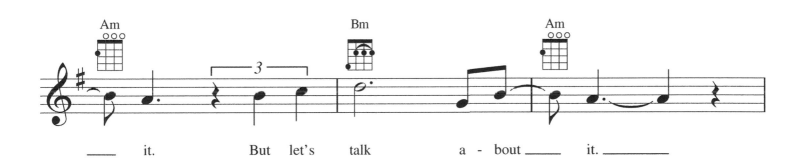

___ it. But let's talk a - bout ___ it. _____

Oh, would-n't it ___ be _____ nice? _____

Little Deuce Coupe

Music by Brian Wilson
Words by Roger Christian

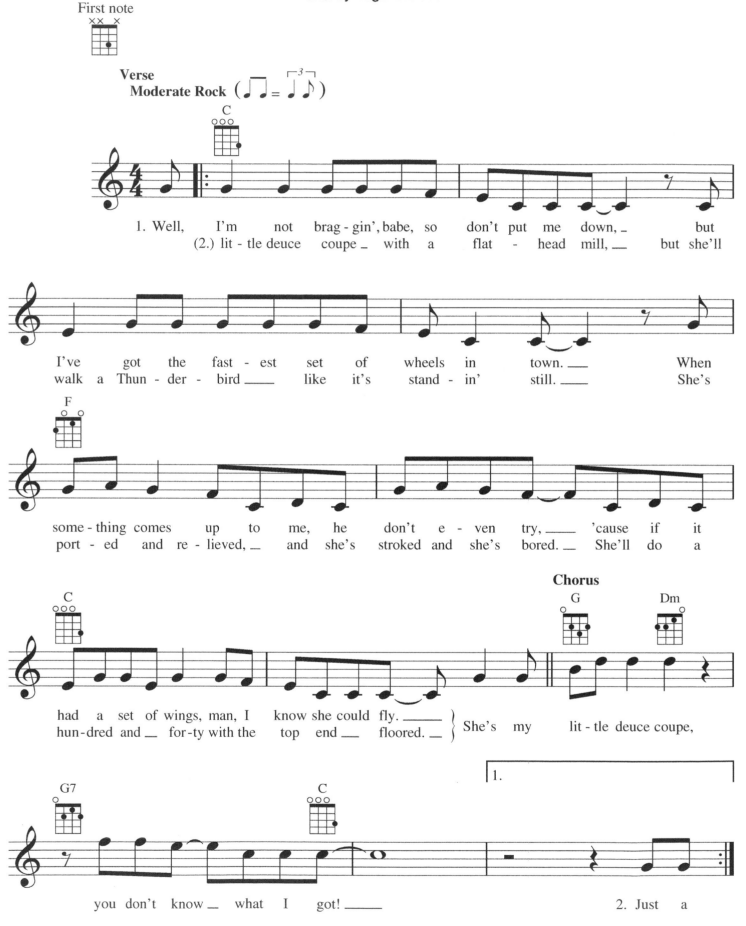

Bridge

C7   F

She's got a com-pe-ti-tion clutch, with four on the floor. _ Yeah, she

C7   F

purrs like a kit-ten till the lake pipes roar. _ And if that ain't e-nough to make you

D7   G7

flip your wig, _ there's one more thing: I've got the pink slip, dad-dy! 3. And

Verse

C

com-in' off the line when the light turns green, _ well, she blows 'em out-ta the wa-ter like you've

F

nev-er seen. _ I get pushed out of shape, _ and it's hard to steer _ when

Outro-Chorus

C   G   Dm

I get rub-ber in-a all four gears. _ She's my lit-tle deuce coupe,

G7   C

you don't know _ what I got! _____

Sloop John B

Words and Music by Brian Wilson

Chorus

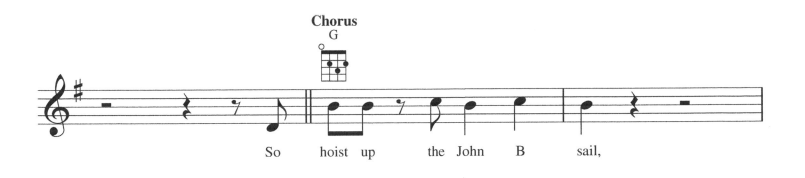

So hoist up the John B sail,

see how the main sail set. Call for the cap - tain a -

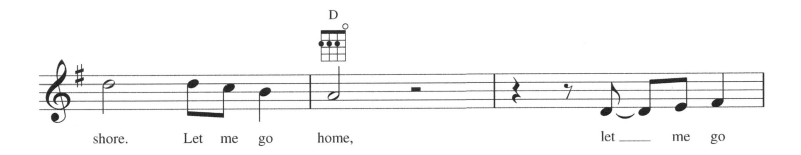

shore. Let me go home, let ____ me go

home. I wan - na go home, oh

yeah. Well, I feel so broke _ up, I wan - na go

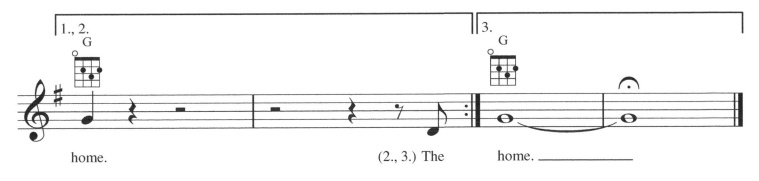

home. (2., 3.) The home. ____

Surfer Girl

Written by Brian Wilson

Surfin' Safari

Words and Music by Brian Wilson and Mike Love

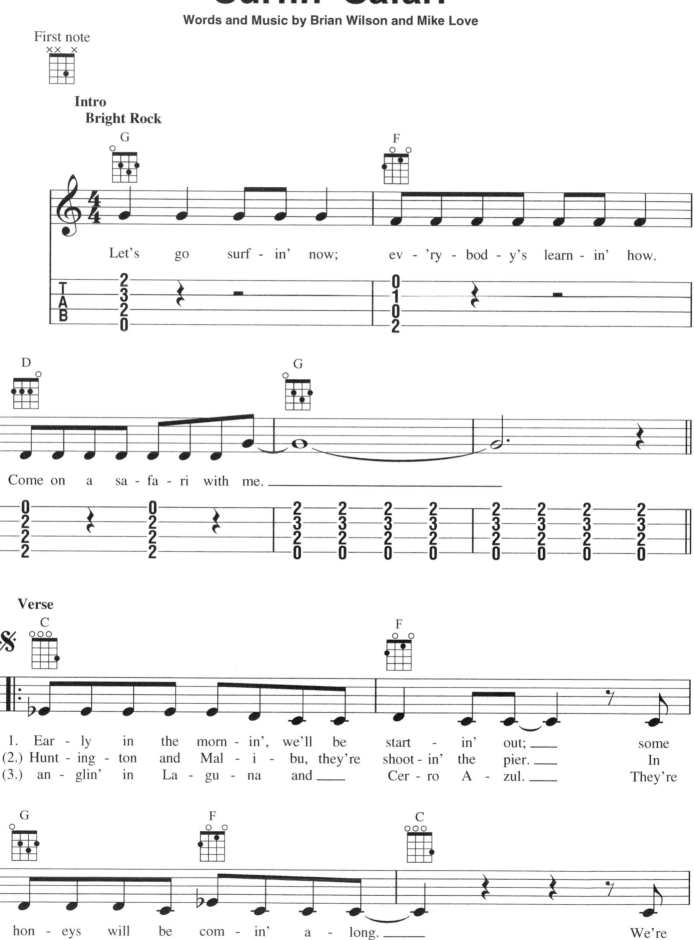

load - in' up our wood - y with the boards in - side   and
go - in' on sa - fa - ri to the is - lands this year. ___ So if you're
surf - in's run - nin' wild; it's get - tin' big - ger ev - 'ry day, from Ha -

Chorus

head - in' out sing - in' our song. ___
com - in', get read - y to go. ___   Come on, ba - by,
wai - i to the shores of Pe - ru. ___

wait and see, ___ yes. I'm gon - na take you surf - in' with me. ___ Come on a -

long, surf ba - by, wait and see, ___ yes. I'm gon - na take you surf - in' with me. ___

To Coda

Let's go surf - in' now; ev - 'ry - bod - y's learn - in' how. Come on a sa - fa - ri with me. ___

Coda

1.   2.

D.S. al Coda

_____   2. In ___   3. They're   _____

43

Surfin' U.S.A.

Words and Music by Chuck Berry

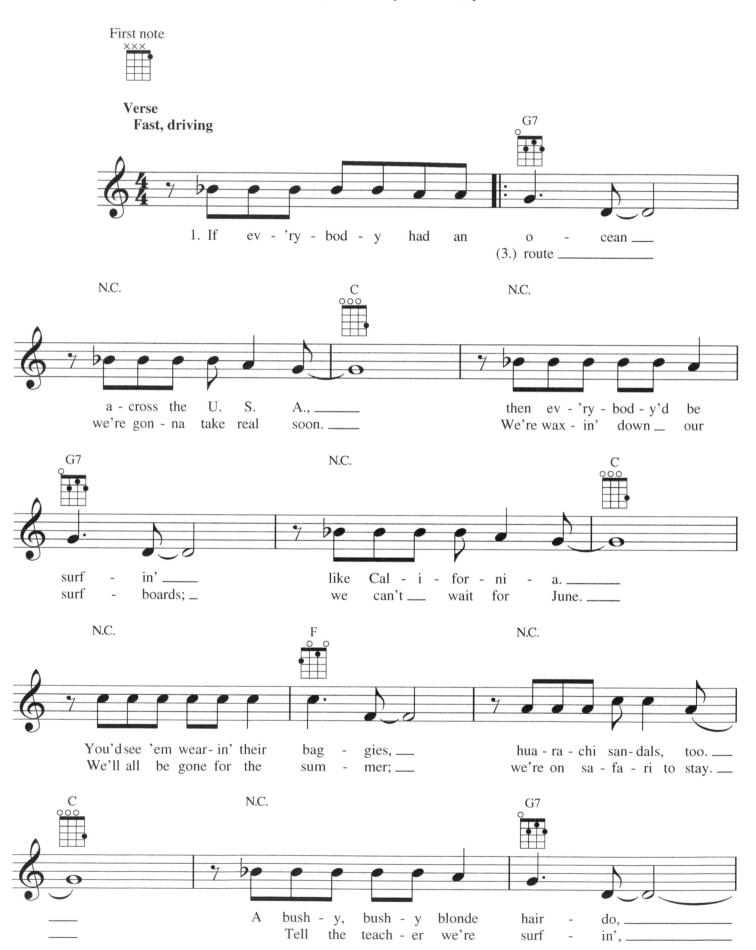

1. If ev - 'ry - bod - y had an o - cean _____
(3.) route _____

a - cross the U. S. A., _____
we're gon - na take real soon. _____

then ev - 'ry - bod - y'd be
We're wax - in' down _ our

surf - in' _____
surf - boards; _

like Cal - i - for - ni - a. _____
we can't _ wait for June. _____

You'd see 'em wear - in' their bag - gies, __
We'll all be gone for the sum - mer; _

hua - ra - chi san - dals, too. _
we're on sa - fa - ri to stay. _

A bush - y, bush - y blonde hair - do, _____
Tell the teach - er we're surf - in', _____

surf - in' U. S.   A.
surf - in' U. S.   A.

2. You'll catch 'em surf - in' at
4. At Hag - gar - ty's ___ and

Verse

Del   Mar, ___   Ven - tu - ra Coun - ty   line, _____
Swa - mi's, ___   Pa - cif - ic Pal - i - sades, _____

___ San - ta Cruz   and   Tres - sels, ___   Aus - tra - lia's Nar - a - bine. ___
___ San O - no - fre and   Sun - set, ___   Re - don - do Beach, L.   A. ___

___   All   o - ver Man - hat - tan ___
___   All   o - ver La   Jo - lla, ___

and down Do - he - ny   Way, ___   ev - 'ry - bod - y's gone   surf - in', _____
at Wai - a - me - a   Bay, ___   ev - 'ry - bod - y's gone   surf - in', _____

1.   N.C.   2.

___ surf - in' U. S.   A. _____
___ surf - in' U. S.   A. _____

3. We'll all be plan - nin' out a

When I Grow Up
(To Be a Man)

Words and Music by Brian Wilson and Mike Love

The Best Collections for Ukulele

The Best Songs Ever
70 songs have now been arranged for ukulele. Includes: Always • Bohemian Rhapsody • Memory • My Favorite Things • Over the Rainbow • Piano Man • What a Wonderful World • Yesterday • You Raise Me Up • and more.
00282413........$17.99

Campfire Songs for Ukulele
30 favorites to sing as you roast marshmallows and strum your uke around the campfire. Includes: God Bless the U.S.A. • Hallelujah • The House of the Rising Sun • I Walk the Line • Puff the Magic Dragon • Wagon Wheel • You Are My Sunshine • and more.
00129170 ....$14.99

The Daily Ukulele
arr. Liz and Jim Beloff
Strum a different song everyday with easy arrangements of 365 of your favorite songs in one big songbook! Includes favorites by the Beatles, Beach Boys, and Bob Dylan, folk songs, pop songs, kids' songs, Christmas carols, and Broadway and Hollywood tunes, all with a spiral binding for ease of use.
00240356 Original Edition.................$39.99
00240681 Leap Year Edition $39.99
00119270 Portable Edition $37.50

Disney Hits for Ukulele
Play 23 of your favorite Disney songs on your ukulele. Includes: The Bare Necessities • Cruella De Vil • Do You Want to Build a Snowman? • Kiss the Girl • Lava • Let It Go • Once upon a Dream • A Whole New World • and more.
00151250 ....$16.99

Also available:
00291547 **Disney Fun Songs for Ukulele** ...$16.99
00701708 **Disney Songs for Ukulele**.......$14.99
00334696 **First 50 Disney Songs on Ukulele** .$16.99

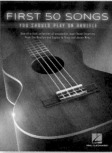

First 50 Songs You Should Play on Ukulele
An amazing collec-tion of 50 accessible, must-know favorites: Edelweiss • Hey, Soul Sister • I Walk the Line • I'm Yours • Imagine • Over the Rainbow • Peaceful Easy Feeling • The Rainbow Connection • Riptide • more.
00149250 ....$16.99

Also available:
00292082 **First 50 Melodies on Ukulele** ...$15.99
00289029 **First 50 Songs on Solo Ukulele**..$15.99
00347437 **First 50 Songs to Strum on Uke** .$16.99

40 Most Streamed Songs for Ukulele
40 top hits that sound great on uke! Includes: Despacito • Feel It Still • Girls like You • Happier • Havana • High Hopes • The Middle • Perfect • 7 Rings • Shallow • Shape of You • Something Just like This • Stay • Sucker • Sunflower • Sweet but Psycho • Thank U, Next • There's Nothing Holdin' Me Back • Without Me • and more!
00298113 ....$17.99

The 4 Chord Songbook
With just 4 chords, you can play 50 hot songs on your ukulele! Songs include: Brown Eyed Girl • Do Wah Diddy Diddy • Hey Ya! • Ho Hey • Jessie's Girl • Let It Be • One Love • Stand by Me • Toes • With or Without You • and many more.
00142050........$16.99

Also available:
00141143 **The 3-Chord Songbook**........$16.99

Pop Songs for Kids
30 easy pop favorites for kids to play on uke, including: Brave • Can't Stop the Feeling! • Feel It Still • Fight Song • Happy • Havana • House of Gold • How Far I'll Go • Let It Go • Remember Me (Ernesto de la Cruz) • Rewrite the Stars • Roar • Shake It Off • Story of My Life • What Makes You Beautiful • and more.
00284415 ....$16.99

Simple Songs for Ukulele
50 favorites for standard G-C-E-A ukulele tuning, including: All Along the Watchtower • Can't Help Falling in Love • Don't Worry, Be Happy • Ho Hey • I'm Yours • King of the Road • Sweet Home Alabama • You Are My Sunshine • and more.
00156815........$14.99

Also available:
00276644 **More Simple Songs for Ukulele** .$14.99

Top Hits of 2020
18 uke-friendly tunes of 2020 are featured in this collection of melody, lyric and chord arrangements in standard G-C-E-A tuning. Includes: Adore You (Harry Styles) • Before You Go (Lewis Capaldi) • Cardigan (Taylor Swift) • Daisies (Katy Perry) • I Dare You (Kelly Clarkson) • Level of Concern (twenty one pilots) • No Time to Die (Billie Eilish) • Rain on Me (Lady Gaga feat. Ariana Grande) • Say So (Doja Cat) • and more.
00355553...........................$14.99

Also available:
00302274 **Top Hits of 2019** $14.99

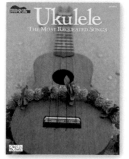

Ukulele: The Most Requested Songs
Strum & Sing Series
Cherry Lane Music
Nearly 50 favorites all expertly arranged for ukulele! Includes: Bubbly • Build Me Up, Buttercup • Cecilia • Georgia on My Mind • Kokomo • L-O-V-E • Your Body Is a Wonderland • and more.
02501453 ....$14.99

The Ultimate Ukulele Fake Book
Uke enthusiasts will love this giant, spiral-bound collection of over 400 songs for uke! Includes: Crazy • Dancing Queen • Downtown • Fields of Gold • Happy • Hey Jude • 7 Years • Summertime • Thinking Out Loud • Thriller • Wagon Wheel • and more.
00175500 9" x 12" Edition $45.00
00319997 5.5" x 8.5" Edition $39.99